Who Was
Steve Jobs?

Who Was
Steve Jobs?

By Pam Pollack and Meg Belviso
Illustrated by John O'Brien

Grosset & Dunlap
An Imprint of Penguin Group (USA) Inc.

To Reo and Hiro, who light up my life—PDP
To Olivia and Melissa, insanely great iNieces—MB
For Linda—JO

GROSSET & DUNLAP
Published by the Penguin Group
Penguin Group (USA) Inc., 375 Hudson Street, New York, New York 10014, USA
Penguin Group (Canada), 90 Eglinton Avenue East, Suite 700,
Toronto, Ontario M4P 2Y3, Canada (a division of Pearson Penguin Canada Inc.)
Penguin Books Ltd, 80 Strand, London WC2R 0RL, England
Penguin Ireland, 25 St Stephen's Green, Dublin 2, Ireland
(a division of Penguin Books Ltd)
Penguin Group (Australia), 707 Collins Street, Melbourne, Victoria 3008, Australia
(a division of Pearson Australia Group Pty Ltd)
Penguin Books India Pvt Ltd, 11 Community Centre,
Panchsheel Park, New Delhi–110 017, India
Penguin Group (NZ), 67 Apollo Drive, Rosedale, Auckland 0632, New Zealand
(a division of Pearson New Zealand Ltd)
Penguin Books (South Africa), Rosebank Office Park, 181 Jan Smuts Avenue,
Parktown North 2193, South Africa
Penguin China, B7 Jiaming Center, 27 East Third Ring Road North,
Chaoyang District, Beijing 100020, China

Penguin Books Ltd, Registered Offices: 80 Strand, London WC2R 0RL, England

Text copyright © 2012 by Pam Pollack and Meg Belviso. Illustrations copyright
© 2012 by John O'Brien. Cover illustration copyright © 2012 by Nancy Harrison.
Published by Grosset & Dunlap, a division of Penguin Young Readers Group,
345 Hudson Street, New York, New York 10014. GROSSET & DUNLAP is a
trademark of Penguin Group (USA) Inc. Printed in the U.S.A.

Library of Congress Control Number: 2011049209.

ISBN (pbk): 978-0-448-46211-0   16 15 14 13 12 11 10 9 8
ISBN (HC): 978-0-448-47940-8   10 9 8 7 6 5 4 3 2 1

Contents

Who Was
Steve Jobs?

Steve Jobs always loved machines. His father repaired machines for a living. As a child, Steve loved to watch his dad build and fix things.

When Steve grew up, he started a company that built machines. Not just any machines, but a machine Steve was sure would soon become part of daily life, just like cars and TV sets. What was this machine?

A personal computer.

Today, millions of people own personal computers. But back in the 1970s nobody did.

The first modern computer came out in 1938. A computer built in 1946 was as big as a room! When Steve was a kid, computers were still too big and complicated for the average person to use. The government used them to gather information.

Steve was going to change that. Steve and his friend Steve Wozniak started Apple Computers in the Jobses' garage. Their computer, the Apple II, was the hit of a West Coast computer fair in 1977.

Why?

It looked fun to use.

In 1979, Steve visited the research center of the tech company Xerox. It was in Palo Alto, California. He walked around, looking at the new computers the engineers were working on.

"What's that?" Steve asked one man. He pointed to a small gadget by a computer. When the engineer moved the gadget with his hand, an arrow on the computer screen moved, too.

"This is a point-and-click graphical user interface," the man explained. That sure was a complicated name for a gadget that did something very simple—and very amazing. Every time the man moved the pointer to a picture on the screen and clicked, it opened a program on the computer.

Steve stared at the little gadget.

In 1979, computers were operated by punching in keys on a keyboard. To work the computer, you had to know

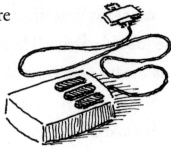

the right keys to push. This little gadget made using the computer so much easier. Steve couldn't believe it. He imagined having something similar for his computers.

"When are you going to sell it?" he asked the engineer.

"We're not," he said. "It's fun, but there's no market for it."

Steve Jobs knew differently. As he stared at the little gadget, he could see the future rolling out in front of him. Billions of people pointing and clicking on their home computers. He would have to improve the gadget. He would make it better. And he wouldn't call it a "point-and-click graphical user interface." He would call it by its friendlier nickname: the mouse.

That day, Steve knew the world was going to change. And he, Steve Jobs, was going to make it happen.

EARLY COMPUTERS

AS ELECTRONIC TECHNOLOGY AND COMPUTERS ADVANCE, THEY GET SMALLER AND SMALLER. A COMPUTER YOU HOLD IN YOUR HAND TODAY CAN DO MORE THAN A COMPUTER THAT SAT ON A DESK TEN YEARS AGO.

THE FIRST COMMERCIAL COMPUTER PRODUCED IN THE UNITED STATES WAS THE UNIVERSAL AUTOMATIC COMPUTER—OR UNIVAC—IN 1951. IT WEIGHED 29,000 POUNDS AND TOOK UP MORE THAN 42.5 SQUARE YARDS OF FLOOR SPACE. YET IT ONLY PERFORMED 1,905 OPERATIONS PER SECOND. TODAY, AN IPAD CAN PERFORM 1.65 BILLION OPERATIONS IN THE SAME SECOND.

Chapter 1
Growing Up in the Valley

In 1954, Joanne Schieble was a graduate student at the University of Wisconsin. She fell in love with a teaching assistant. He was from Syria. And his name was Abdulfattah Jandali. They were young and had no money. So when Joanne learned she was going to have a baby, they decided to put the baby up for adoption.

Paul and Clara Jobs wanted a child very much. They adopted the couple's baby and named him Steven Paul Jobs. He was born on February 24, 1955. Three years after Steve was born, the Jobses

adopted a little girl, Patti. Steve liked his little sister. But they didn't have much in common.

The family lived in Mountain View, California. It was a beautiful area full of fruit trees. People called it the Valley of Heart's Delight. But Mountain View was changing. New companies were coming to the area. The companies were trying to develop new electronic equipment. Eventually, the area became known by a different name: Silicon Valley.

SILICON VALLEY

SILICON VALLEY WAS GIVEN ITS NAME BY NEWSPAPERS REPORTING ABOUT THE NEW INDUSTRY SPRINGING UP IN NORTHERN CALIFORNIA. THIS NEW INDUSTRY MADE SEMICONDUCTOR CHIPS. THESE CHIPS COULD CHANNEL ELECTRICITY. THAT MADE THEM VERY IMPORTANT FOR COMPUTERS AND OTHER ELECTRONIC DEVICES. THEY USED SILICON, A VERY FINE SAND, AS A RAW MATERIAL TO MAKE THEM.

Steve loved to help his father work on cars. Paul even made him his own little workbench when Steve was five. He showed

him how to use a hammer and saw. Paul was a mechanical whiz, and he passed on his love of gadgets to his son. A neighbor gave Steve his first Heathkit—Steve made radio transistors with it.

In 1968, when he was thirteen, Steve discovered a part was missing from one of his kits. The kit was made by Hewlett-Packard, a big company in Silicon Valley that developed and made parts for computers. Steve got a phone book and looked up the number of Bill Hewlett. He was one of the founders of the company. Steve called him to complain. By the time they got off the phone, Hewlett had offered Steve a summer job and promised him a bagful of machine parts. What was Steve's answer?

Yes, of course!

Steve also joined Hewlett-Packard's Explorer Club. It offered lectures to kids interested in electronics. At one lecture, Steve saw a computer for the first time.

At school, Steve hung around with other kids who loved electronics. He also had a girlfriend, Chrisann Brennan. Through the kids in his computer club, Steve met Steve Wozniak who was several years older. "Woz" had an amazing talent for making things. He was going to a local college and designing computers as a hobby.

STEVE WOZNIAK

When Steve graduated from high school in 1972, he enrolled at Reed College in Oregon. There was only one problem: Steve couldn't pay for college. So Steve went to the dean of Reed. He asked if he could live in the dorms and sit in on classes for free. Steve wouldn't ever get a degree, but he would learn about subjects he was interested in.

Why would the dean agree to that?

Like Bill Hewlett at Hewlett-Packard, the dean was impressed by Steve. And he did say yes. Within a week, Steve was attending classes. He studied eastern religions and calligraphy, which was the art of fine handwriting. It wasn't an easy life. Steve slept on the floor of his friends' rooms.

He collected Coke bottles for spending money. And he depended on local charities for food.

Steve stayed at Reed for eighteen months. He'd had enough of college life. He wanted to go to India. To get money for the trip, he took a job at Atari. It made some of the very first computer games. His friend Woz was already working there. By summer, Steve had saved enough to go to India. After the trip, he came back to Atari.

Personal computers in 1976—if you saw them at all—looked like airplane cockpits full of switches and lights. Woz had created a circuit board for an easy-to-use personal computer. A person could type in a command, Woz explained to Steve, and the computer would follow the command on a TV screen in front of the person.

Woz thought of it as a neat project. Steve thought it could be more than that. He thought they should leave Atari and start a whole new company.

PONG

ATARI'S *PONG* WAS ONE OF THE FIRST VIDEO GAMES. *PONG* HAD A TV-SIZED SCREEN THAT WAS INSIDE SOMETHING ABOUT THE SIZE OF A PHONE BOOTH. PLAYING *PONG* WAS LIKE PLAYING ELECTRONIC PING-PONG. BY MODERN STANDARDS, IT'S NOT VERY EXCITING. BUT FOR PEOPLE IN 1972, IT WAS CUTTING EDGE! BY PRESSING BUTTONS, TWO PLAYERS HIT A BALL BACK AND FORTH ACROSS THE SCREEN. THE SUCCESS OF *PONG* INSPIRED OTHER COMPUTER GAMES THAT BECAME MORE AND MORE SOPHISTICATED, LEADING TO THE GAMES WE HAVE TODAY.

Chapter 2
The Birth of Apple

Apple Computers officially went into business on April Fools' Day 1976. Steve was living with his girlfriend, Chrisann Brennan, who was an artist. The new company's "office" was Steve's parents' garage. All the work was done there. They planned to sell Woz's circuit boards to people who wanted to build their own home computers.

They built a sample computer with Woz's circuit board to show how it worked. They called the computer the Apple.

Why did they pick that name?

Well, Steve ate a lot of fruit, sometimes nothing but fruit. He thought the apple was the best fruit of all. It was perfect, just like he wanted his computer to be.

They showed the computer with Woz's circuit board to the owner of a local electronics store. He said, "I can't see stocking just circuit boards. Not that many people know how to put together a whole computer. But if you could sell me computers like this one, I think people would buy them."

The store owner offered Steve twenty-five thousand dollars for fifty Apple computers. He'd pay in cash when he had the machines.

"Deal," said Steve, even though making so many computers would cost a lot of money— money they didn't have.

But Steve came up with an idea. He went to an electronic supply store. He persuaded the store

to give him the parts to make the computers.
Steve couldn't pay for the parts right then. But he
promised to pay the store back later.

Steve was awfully good at persuading people to
do what he asked. The store said yes.

Each Apple computer cost two hundred twenty
dollars to make. Each Apple computer was sold to

the electronics store for five hundred dollars. So even after Steve and Woz paid back the electronic supply store, they made a very big profit.

If most people today saw that Apple computer, they would be stunned. It didn't come with a keyboard, monitor, or case. Steve and Woz knew they could do better. What if they made a computer that came with everything, so a person could just take it out of the box and use it right away? Steve bet they could sell a lot. He and Woz got to work on making such a computer—the Apple II.

Woz and Steve had big dreams for the Apple II. Woz wanted it to have color, sound, and sharp, crisp graphics. Steve wanted it to accept floppy disks that could store extra information. He wanted to encase the computer in molded plastic. At the time, plastic was much more expensive than metal

FLOPPY DISK

or wood. But Steve thought plastic looked cool and modern. And how a computer looked was important. If it looked good, people would want it.

Steve found an investor who gave them enough money to finish the Apple II in time for a computer fair in San Francisco. They took models to display at the fair. There was a lot that was new and different about the Apple II.

While Woz was working on the computer, Steve hired a designer to come up with a new logo. A logo is a picture that stands for a company.

A good logo helps people remember the company. For instance, General Electric's logo is a lightbulb. Steve wanted an apple to represent Apple. Apple's apple logo looked fun; it was rainbow colored and had a bite taken out of it.

Woz and Steve's hard work paid off. People visiting the West Coast Computer Faire in 1977 passed many displays of bulky computers that looked like high school science projects. Then they saw the Apple II. Here was a computer that featured color, clear graphics, and sound. For years afterward, every other computer company would copy it.

All the technological improvements were the work of Steve Wozniak. But Steve Jobs's design ideas were just as important. He had learned from his dad to insist on perfection. Even wires inside the computer, wires that nobody could see, had to be perfectly straight. This was the way Steve's dad built machines, and Steve would, too. Everything had to look simple and beautiful.

Chapter 3
Up and Down—and Out

By 1978, Apple was making money. The
company grew quickly. Steve wanted all Apple
products to run smoothly. But working with Steve
was not easy. Small mistakes made him angry.
Sometimes Steve yelled at his employees—even

making them cry. And if he didn't get what he wanted, he often burst into tears himself. Employees tried to please Steve. But often Steve couldn't explain what he wanted. He simply said, "I'll know it when I see it."

In 1979, Apple started to make a new home computer that used a mouse. The company hired thousands of employees. Steve worked long hours, and he expected his employees to work hard, too. He was so devoted to Apple that he didn't have time for anything else. His girlfriend, Chrisann, had a daughter, Lisa, on May 17, 1978. Steve refused to have anything to do with his baby. He had no interest in a family.

In 1980, Steve Jobs became the youngest person in history to make *Fortune* magazine's list of top Americans in business. He was twenty-five years old, and he was a millionaire.

Then in 1981, something terrible happened. Woz's private plane crashed. It took months for

Woz to recuperate. He never returned to work for
Apple full-time.

STEVE WOZNIAK

LIKE STEVE JOBS, STEVE WOZNIAK GREW UP IN WHAT WOULD BECOME THE SILICON VALLEY. WOZ WAS BORN ON AUGUST 11, 1950. HIS FATHER WAS AN ENGINEER AT LOCKHEED MARTIN, WHICH MADE MISSILES AND SATELLITES. EVEN AS A KID, WOZ HAD A TALENT FOR BUILDING

STEVE WOZNIAK

AND DESIGNING ELECTRONICS. IN JUNIOR HIGH, HE AND HIS FATHER CREATED AN ELECTRONIC TIC-TAC-TOE GAME FOR A SCIENCE FAIR.

AT APPLE, WOZ CREATED ELECTRONIC DEVICES THAT WORKED IN NEW AND BETTER WAYS. BUT HE HAD LITTLE INTEREST IN MAKING MONEY. IT WAS HIS FRIEND STEVE JOBS WHO FIGURED OUT HOW TO MARKET COMPUTERS AND MAKE THEM MORE APPEALING TO THE AVERAGE PERSON. ALTHOUGH THEY DIDN'T REMAIN CLOSE FRIENDS, WOZ AND STEVE JOBS ALWAYS STAYED IN TOUCH. MARRIED FOUR TIMES WITH THREE CHILDREN, WOZ STILL LIVES IN CALIFORNIA IN THE TOWN OF LOS GATOS.

It was a big change for Steve. He and Woz had worked together so closely. Working with other engineers wasn't nearly as satisfying. Steve wasn't happy with the company's next computer. It was too big and too expensive. Nobody wanted to pay $10,000 for a computer.

Steve had already set his sights on a new idea: It was a computer called the Macintosh. A Macintosh is a type of apple. The Macintosh would change the world. Steve was sure of it. He handpicked a team of engineers to build it. They worked in a separate building. A pirate flag flew

on top. "It's better to be a pirate than to join the navy," he said. By this, he meant sometimes it was good to break rules and think in a different way.

Steve broke all sorts of rules. He didn't like to wear shoes. He only ate fruit. He thought his diet made him so clean that he didn't need to bathe often. A lot of people didn't like to work with him because he smelled bad.

Despite his strange ways, Steve could convince people to do things that seemed impossible. An Apple employee made up a name for Steve's power. He called it the "reality distortion field (RDF)." Steve's RDF made people believe that anything Steve wanted was possible if they worked hard enough.

One thing Steve really wanted was to hire a smart businessman at Apple. He thought the best person was John Sculley. Sculley was the head of the Pepsi-Cola company. He wasn't sure if he should go to Apple. So Steve asked him, "Do you want to sell sugared water for the rest of your life, or do you want to come with me and change the world?" Here was Steve's RDF at work! Like many before him, Sculley ended up doing what Steve wanted. He came to work for Apple.

In 1984, Steve introduced the Macintosh to the world. It was the computer "for the rest of us," according to the ads. That meant it was not just for scientists and superbrainy "tech" nerds. It was easy to use and friendly to look at. It incorporated everything Steve had learned about sleek design— it even used the knowledge of calligraphy he'd learned about back at Reed. When people typed on their Mac computers, Steve wanted the letters to be beautiful. He spent a lot of time choosing how much space would be in between letters. The Mac offered several different fonts, or writing styles. Each one had slightly different letters. This made typing on the Mac fun.

The Macintosh was far from perfect. It didn't have very much memory, and there was no way of adding on more. One man at Apple called it "a Honda with a one-gallon gas tank." But in Steve's words, the Macintosh computer was "insanely great."

The first Macintosh commercial ran during the Super Bowl in 1984. By the end of the game, everyone wanted to know more about the Mac.

The Mac sold amazingly well—for a short time.

Why wasn't it a giant hit?

People were just not as interested in buying home computers as Steve had expected. And not all customers who did want a home computer bought Apple computers. Many bought computers from IBM or Microsoft.

John Sculley was not happy at Apple. For him, the disappointing Macintosh sales were proof that Steve's ideas were wrong. Regular people would never need or want home computers. If Apple was to survive, Sculley said it should make computers for businesses. They should make Apple computers that worked with products made by other computer companies.

Steve hated that idea. He wanted customers

SUPER BOWL AD

1984 WAS THE YEAR THE MACINTOSH COMPUTER WAS INTRODUCED. 1984 IS ALSO THE TITLE OF A NOVEL BY GEORGE ORWELL. THE NOVEL TAKES PLACE IN A WORLD WHERE "BIG BROTHER" PUNISHES ANYONE WHO STEPS OUT OF LINE. APPLE'S FIRST MACINTOSH COMMERCIAL SHOWED A SIMILAR WORLD. EVERYONE WORE THE SAME GRAY CLOTHES AND TOOK ORDERS FROM A "BIG BROTHER" CHARACTER ON A GIANT TV SCREEN—UNTIL A BRIGHTLY COLORED RUNNER, REPRESENTING APPLE, SMASHED THE SCREEN THE WAY STEVE JOBS HOPED THE MACINTOSH WOULD SMASH INTO THE COMPUTER INDUSTRY. THE COMMERCIAL WAS

DIRECTED BY RIDLEY SCOTT, THE DIRECTOR OF HIT SCI-FI FILMS INCLUDING *ALIEN* AND *BLADE RUNNER*. IN 2004, APPLE RERAN THE AD. ONLY THIS TIME THE RUNNER WAS LISTENING TO AN IPOD.

to run Apple products on Apple computers. He didn't want outside programs anywhere near the Macintosh.

Steve didn't like someone else telling him what to do. He had hired Sculley hoping that the older man would teach him how to run a big company. After that, Steve expected Sculley to hand the reins back to him. Instead, Sculley wanted to make more changes.

Every big company has a group of outside people that give advice to the company. This kind of group is called a board. A company's board can also hire and fire the head of the company. Steve tried to get Apple's board to fire Sculley. That didn't happen. Instead, the board replaced Steve as head of the Macintosh!

It was May 1985. Steve Jobs lost all the power he had at Apple. He was moved to a new office across the street from most of the other Apple buildings. He rarely saw other employees. Steve

nicknamed his new office "Siberia," which is a
remote part of Russia. It made him so unhappy,
he started spending less time at work. In
September of that year, Steve left Apple.

What would Steve Jobs do next?

Chapter 4
What's NeXT?

By 1985, families were starting to buy computers for their homes. College students regularly worked on computers to do schoolwork. Steve Jobs wasn't finished with the computer business. He wanted to show the people at Apple that they were wrong about him. He started a new company. He called it NeXT because it was going to be the next step in computers. He hoped to sell his new computers to colleges across the country. Students and professors would work with them.

But Steve's plan for the perfect computer was expensive. He hired a famous designer to create a logo for his new company. The logo cost one hundred thousand dollars!

NeXT lost ten million dollars in three years. Steve put more and more of his own money into the company. But nobody was buying the computers he made. They were too expensive. Colleges couldn't afford computers that cost sixty-five hundred dollars a piece.

Nothing at NeXT was going the way Steve hoped. But he struggled on. He tried to run the company in a different way from Apple. He called employees "members" of the NeXT "community." He paid people according to how long they had worked at NeXT. He gave frequent raises. Steve could be generous, but he was still the same demanding boss he had always been.

Steve's family life was changing. In 1986, his mother died. Although Steve considered the Jobses to be his real parents, he was interested to know about the couple who gave birth to him.

A doctor's name was on Steve's birth certificate. Through that doctor, he learned that his mother's

maiden name was Joanne Schieble. She had
married his father Abdulfattah Jandali in 1956
and had a daughter, Mona. They weren't married
for long. Joanne then married a man whose last
name was Simpson. Her daughter went by the
name Mona Simpson. Steve met his mother and

new sister. Mona was a novelist.
Even though Steve and Mona
hadn't grown up together,
they became close. Mona
also encouraged Steve
to be a part of his
daughter Lisa's life.
Lisa was seven now.

LISA BRENNAN-JOBS

Steve had had many
girlfriends since Chrisann
Brennan. One was the famous
folksinger Joan Baez. Dating Joan Baez was
especially exciting for Steve because she had once
been the girlfriend of one of his favorite singers,
Bob Dylan.

But Steve was in his midthirties and had never
come close to being married.

Then in 1990, Steve gave a lecture at Stanford
University. In the audience was Laurene Powell.
Laurene was a graduate student studying business.

Laurene was so pretty that Steve noticed her right away. Afterward, the two got to talking. Like Steve, Laurene

didn't eat meat and was very smart. They exchanged phone numbers. Steve went out into the parking lot to find his car. He had a business meeting that night. But as he was getting into his car, he thought to himself, "If this was my last day on earth, would I rather spend it at a business meeting or with this woman?" He ran across the parking lot and caught up with Laurene.

The two had dinner together. A year later, they were married in Yosemite National Park.

MONA SIMPSON

MONA SIMPSON IS A WELL-KNOWN NOVELIST. SHE MET HER BROTHER, STEVE, WHILE SHE WAS WORKING ON HER FIRST BOOK, *ANYWHERE BUT HERE*. THE BOOK WENT ON TO WIN AN AWARD GIVEN TO NEW WRITERS. IT WAS LATER MADE INTO A MOVIE STARRING SUSAN SARANDON AND NATALIE PORTMAN. MONA DEDICATED THE BOOK TO HER MOTHER AND HER BROTHER, STEVE. ANOTHER ONE OF HER BOOKS WAS CALLED *A REGULAR GUY*. STEVE THOUGHT THE MAIN CHARACTER SEEMED TOO MUCH LIKE HIM. BUT STEVE AND MONA REMAINED CLOSE UNTIL THE END OF HIS LIFE.

Steve and Laurene's first child, Reed Paul Jobs, was born in September 1991. He was named after Reed College.

Things still weren't going well at NeXT. But Steve was discovering that life was more than just business. His father, the person he was closest to, died in 1993. Steve had loved the time he spent working on cars with his father. He wanted his children to have happy memories of him, too. His now-teenage daughter, Lisa, came to live with him for the first time. Even if he was never a success again, Steve thought, he would have a happy family life.

STEVE JOBS'S OTHER FATHER

WHEN STEVE JOBS WAS LOOKING FOR HIS BIOLOGICAL MOTHER, HE DECIDED THAT HE DIDN'T WANT TO MEET HIS FATHER. BUT IN FACT, HE HAD ALREADY MET HIM! ABDULFATTAH JANDALI RAN A RESTAURANT IN SILICON VALLEY. STEVE HAD EATEN THERE SEVERAL TIMES. HE HAD MET ABDULFATTAH, BUT NEITHER MAN KNEW THEY WERE RELATED.

LATER ON, MONA SIMPSON MET HER FATHER AFTER MANY YEARS OF NOT SEEING HIM. HE TALKED ABOUT HIS OLD RESTAURANT. HE TOLD MONA THAT IT WAS THE BEST IN THE SILICON VALLEY. "EVERYONE USED TO EAT THERE," HE SAID. "EVEN STEVE JOBS! HE WAS A GREAT TIPPER!" IT WAS MONA WHO TOLD ABDULFATTAH THAT STEVE WAS HIS SON! HE NEVER SAW STEVE AGAIN, BUT HE WAS PROUD TO HAVE SERVED THE APPLE FOUNDER.

Chapter 5
To Infinity and Beyond

Steve Jobs admired anyone who did something new and different. He was a huge fan of George Lucas, the director of the Star Wars movies. In 1980, Steve bought out a theater for a night so that everyone at Apple could see *The Empire Strikes Back* together.

In 1986, Steve finally got to work with Lucas. He became an owner in Lucas's computer graphics company. Steve named the company Pixar.

GEORGE LUCAS

Lucas's company had created a new kind of animation using a computer. Steve hoped to sell this program to animators. But it was too expensive. Artists didn't think they needed it. Pixar was losing a lot of money. In fact, Steve put more than fifty million dollars of his own money to keep the company going. He only paid himself fifty dollars a year for his salary.

In 1991, Steve laid off most of Pixar's staff. One person he didn't lay off was John Lasseter. Lasseter had made a number of short computer-animated films. The films were the best way

to show customers what the program could do.
Lasseter's short movies were good—one of them,
Tin Toy, won an Oscar for Best Animated Short
Film in 1989.

Despite the Oscar, Pixar was a failure—a big
failure. NeXT and Pixar were seen as proof that
Steve was nothing more than a slick salesman.
Even his early success with the Apple II was
considered a fluke. Woz was the genius, people
thought. Not Steve.

In 1991, the Walt Disney Company wanted to hire Lasseter. But he said no. And once again, Steve came up with one of his unusual offers. He convinced Disney to give Pixar enough money to make three full-length animated movies. All the animation would be done on a computer. This had never been done before. Perhaps Disney fell under the influence of Steve's famous "reality distortion field." By this time, all the people at Pixar knew about the power of Steve's RDF. They even had a signal for it. In meetings, when someone was getting sucked into the RDF, people would tug on their ears.

The deal with Disney wouldn't make Pixar much money—if the movies were hits, Disney would get most of the profits. But it gave Steve a chance to get Pixar movies made.

Animated movies take a long time to make. Pixar started work on its first full-length movie in 1991. But it did not come out for another four years. Meanwhile, Steve kept pouring funds into both Pixar and NeXT. In 1993, Steve had to lay off most of the workers at NeXT. He felt so helpless and so awful that he stopped going in to work. He spent his days at home with Reed. He loved being with his little boy who, he said, had Laurene's kindness.

Chapter 6
Return to Apple

Steve didn't know it, but he was about to be
rescued by a cowboy and a spaceman.

Inspired by *Tin Toy*, Pixar's first full-length movie opened in 1995. It was called *Toy Story*. The characters were all toys. A cowboy doll and an astronaut action figure were the stars. *Toy Story* became the most popular movie of the year. Pixar went on to make a dozen hit movies in a row.

COMPUTER ANIMATION

TOY STORY WAS THE FIRST FULL-LENGTH MOVIE TOTALLY ANIMATED ON A COMPUTER. BEFORE TOY STORY, ANIMATED FEATURES WERE DONE IN CEL ANIMATION. THAT MEANT EVERY FRAME OF THE MOVIE HAD TO BE HAND PAINTED ON A TRANSPARENT SHEET (A "CEL"). FOR A CHARACTER TO JUST MOVE A HAND UP AND DOWN TOOK MANY CELS. FOR YEARS, ANIMATORS WERE USING COMPUTERS TO HELP THEM ANIMATE FASTER.

A SCRIPT IS GIVEN TO ARTISTS TO BE SKETCHED OUT ONTO STORYBOARDS THAT ARE DISPLAYED LIKE A COMIC BOOK.

THE STORYBOARDS ARE VIDEOTAPED ONTO REELS FOR PLANNING OUT THE FLOW, TIMING, AND LENGTH OF THE FILM.

TOY STORY SHOWED THAT ANIMATORS COULD CREATE EVERYTHING ON A COMPUTER. TRADITIONAL ANIMATION WAS TWO-DIMENSIONAL, LIKE A PAINTING. COMPUTER GENERATED IMAGES (CGI) LOOK THREE-DIMENSIONAL AS IF CHARACTERS ARE REAL AND BEING FILMED BY A CAMERA.

ACTORS RECORD THE CHARACTERS' VOICES.

ARTISTS DESIGN THE CHARACTERS, SETS, AND PROPS. THEY ALSO ADD COLOR.

THE ARTISTS' CHARACTER AND SET DESIGNS
ARE MOLDED INTO THREE-DIMENSIONAL MODELS
WHICH ARE THEN SCANNED ONTO THE COMPUTER.

WITH SPECIAL COMPUTER SOFTWARE THAT CREATES MOVEMENT, THE CHARACTERS ARE CHOREOGRAPHED WITH THE VOICES, MUSIC, AND OTHER SPECIAL EFFECTS INTO A FINISHED FILM.

By 1996, after ten years of struggle, Steve Jobs was a success—a big success. He wasn't a millionaire anymore. He was a billionaire.

Apple, however, the company he had cofounded, was struggling. Apple computers had failed to change with the times. Other computers were just as good and less expensive. Apple computers were slow. They couldn't handle new features that had been developed for computers over the decade. John Sculley, who had forced Steve out, had been himself forced out in 1993. Now the board at Apple wanted Steve back.

For Steve, having the power to do things the way he wanted was more important than having a huge amount of money. He wasn't that interested in buying expensive things. The house where he lived with his family didn't look like the house of a billionaire.

Steve had mixed feelings about returning to Apple. He had bad memories of the way he'd been treated at Apple. He was already the head of a very successful company at Pixar. He and Laurene had a daughter Erin Sienna, born in 1995. Did he really want to take on a struggling company?

If it had been any other company, the answer might have been no. But Apple was his baby. He couldn't just sit by and watch it die.

Steve agreed to act as the head of Apple, but only for a while. Apple had to look for someone else to become his permanent replacement. He gave himself a salary of one dollar per year.

Right away, Steve made big changes. In Boston in 1997, he announced to an audience full of Mac lovers that Apple was going to team up with Microsoft.

Apple and Microsoft were going to work together? This was unheard of! But Steve said

that all Apple computers would use Microsoft's Internet Explorer Web browser.

Behind Steve onstage was a giant TV screen. When Bill Gates, the head of Microsoft, appeared on the screen, the audience booed. But Steve knew that the one-hundred-fifty-million-dollar deal

would help Apple. He was right. The company's value rose.

Steve made other changes. He got rid of products that weren't selling. He cut costs. He laid off so many workers that Apple employees were afraid of riding an elevator with him. They were

scared that they would no longer have a job by the time they got to their floor. Steve still claimed that he was only a temporary CEO. In 1997, he told *TIME* magazine,

"I'm here almost every day, but just for the next few months. I'm really clear on it." But he was making changes for the future.

BILL GATES

BILL GATES BECAME FASCINATED BY COMPUTERS AT ABOUT THE SAME TIME AS STEVE JOBS. HE GREW UP IN SEATTLE AND WENT TO HARVARD UNIVERSITY BUT DID NOT GRADUATE. IN 1974, HE FOUNDED HIS OWN COMPUTER TECHNOLOGY COMPANY, MICROSOFT. IN 1980, MICROSOFT WAS MAKING SOFTWARE FOR IBM COMPUTERS. IBM WAS THE MAIN COMPETITOR OF APPLE. BILL AND STEVE KNEW EACH OTHER. SOMETIMES THEY WERE EVEN FRIENDS. BUT THEY OFTEN DISAGREED.

BILL GATES

IN 1985, MICROSOFT STARTED SELLING WINDOWS, AN OPERATING SYSTEM THAT COULD RUN ON MANY DIFFERENT BRANDS OF COMPUTERS. JUST LIKE APPLE, IT USED A MOUSE TO CLICK ON PICTURES AND TEXT. STEVE ACCUSED BILL OF RIPPING OFF APPLE. BILL REPLIED THAT THEY HAD BOTH TAKEN THE IDEA FROM XEROX. STEVE HAD JUST STOLEN IT FIRST.

BILL STEPPED DOWN AS HEAD OF MICROSOFT IN 2000. EVENTUALLY, HE STARTED WORKING FULL-TIME AT THE CHARITY ORGANIZATION HE RAN WITH HIS WIFE. IT IS THE LARGEST PRIVATE CHARITY IN THE WORLD. IT GIVES MONEY FOR EDUCATION IN THE UNITED STATES. IT WORKS TO END POVERTY AND HUNGER. IT ALSO PROVIDES HEALTH CARE ALL OVER THE WORLD.

Chapter 7
Think Different

In 1997, in cities across America, a series
of posters appeared on buildings, buses, and
billboards. The posters showed photos of famous
people known for doing something new. There
was a poster of Alfred Hitchcock, the famous
movie director. Another poster was of Lucille Ball

and Desi Arnaz, stars of *I Love Lucy*. Another poster showed Jim Henson and Kermit the Frog. In the corner of each poster was the Apple logo and two words: THINK DIFFERENT.

The ad campaign was the brainchild of Steve Jobs. He wanted to show what Apple stood for—new ideas, not the "same old, same old." The posters didn't advertise any particular product. But they told the public to be ready because something exciting was happening at Apple.

What was happening was the iMac—short for Internet Macintosh. This new personal computer was inexpensive and easy to use. In the 1990s, there was a brand-new pastime—surfing the Web. Steve wanted people to surf on iMacs. He also wanted iMacs to look different. The iMac came in a plastic case in five bright colors inspired by Steve's visit to a jelly bean factory: blueberry, grape, lime, strawberry, and tangerine.

Within a year, the iMac became the best-selling computer in the world. That same year, Steve and Laurene had another baby daughter, Eve. Steve's eldest daughter, Lisa, was studying journalism at Harvard University. It was a happy time in Steve's life.

Steve had planned to only stay at Apple for a few months. But in 2000, he became the permanent head. He had too many big plans to leave Apple now.

In May 2001, Apple opened its first stores. Just as Apple computers didn't look like other computers, Apple stores were very different, too. Made with a lot of glass, they looked more like works of art.

Steve oversaw every step of the design of the stores from the floor tiles to the shelves. Every single detail was important to him.

APPLE STORE
FIFTH AVENUE, NYC

APPLE STORE
SHANGHAI

APPLE STORE
LINCOLN ROAD, MIAMI BEACH

At the store's Genius Bar, people could ask questions about problems with their machines and get personal training on their computers.

Steve had put Apple on top of the personal computer market. As he had predicted, people used their computers for work and also for pleasure. Listening to music was something else people did for fun. In the 1990s, most people listened to music on compact discs (CDs). A CD was like a record album. People bought CDs by their favorite groups and played them on CD players. They were about the size of a butter plate and had better sound than a vinyl record album.

But Steve started thinking about something even better. He bought a software program that allowed people to take their favorite songs from a

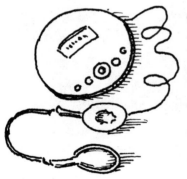

CD and put them on the computer as a digital file. It was called an MP3 file. Once it was on the computer, you didn't need the CD anymore. Steve renamed the program

iTunes. Using iTunes, a person could turn their computer into a personal jukebox.

Other companies created MP3 players. These were portable machines that hooked up to speakers or headphones and played music files. No CD or cassette tape was needed. Steve Jobs decided that Apple had to make its own player.

In October 2001, at a press event in California, Steve reached into his pocket. He pulled out a thin gadget that was smaller than a bar of Hershey's chocolate. "We call it the iPod," he said.

At first, the iPod only worked with Mac computers. But in 2002, Steve agreed to make it work with Microsoft's Windows machines. Now that Windows users could also use the iPod, its sales skyrocketed.

Customers loved the iPod.

People in the music industry did not. Most people got the songs they played on their iPods off CDs. The CD didn't have to be theirs. For instance, they could get songs for free from a friend's CD. Songs could also be "shared" over the Internet.

Nobody in the music industry could figure out how to make people pay for music that they could get for free illegally.

Nobody except Steve. If people could buy music easily and cheaply, he thought they wouldn't mind paying.

Because he could "think different," Steve opened the iTunes Music Store in 2003. It was not a regular store; it wasn't in a building. It was a program you downloaded onto a computer. Using his famous powers of persuasion, he made a deal with many record companies to sell their songs on iTunes for ninety-nine cents a piece.

In the first day it was open, the iTunes store sold two hundred seventy-five thousand songs. It was so easy to order songs. It didn't cost much. Everyone began buying music over the Internet.

STEVE JOBS AND MUSIC

ALTHOUGH STEVE AND WOZ WERE BOTH CRAZY ABOUT COMPUTERS, THEIR FRIENDSHIP REALLY STARTED BECAUSE THEY SHARED THE SAME TASTES IN MUSIC. THEY BOTH LOVED THE SINGER-SONGWRITER BOB DYLAN. STEVE HUNTED FOR RECORDINGS OF DYLAN'S LIVE SHOWS ON REEL-TO-REEL TAPES. STEVE FINALLY MET DYLAN IN PERSON IN 2004. STEVE ALSO LOVED THE BEATLES. SO HE WAS DETERMINED FOR BEATLES' SONGS TO BE SOLD ON ITUNES. IT TOOK YEARS FOR HIM TO COME TO A DEAL WITH THE SURVIVING BAND MEMBERS AND THEIR FAMILIES. FINALLY, IN 2010, BEATLES' SONGS BECAME AVAILABLE ON ITUNES.

Chapter 8
Insanely Great

Apple was back on top and so was Steve. He was still the head of Pixar. He was also helping to raise Reed, Erin, and Eve. Lisa had graduated from Harvard. His wife, Laurene, had founded College Track, a charity that helps kids from poor families get into college.

Steve had many plans for the future. Then
something happened that he could not control.
In 2003, a medical checkup revealed that he had
cancer in his pancreas. His doctors as well as

Laurene and many friends advised Steve to have surgery right away. But as always, Steve wanted to "think different." Steve tried to treat his cancer by changing his diet. But the cancer grew. So in July 2004, he agreed to have surgery to remove the tumor. He told people at Apple he expected to return to work in September.

Steve did return to work. However, he didn't look well. He was losing weight and was pale. People worried that the cancer was growing again. He didn't talk much about being sick. But in 2005, he gave a speech to the graduating class at Stanford University. He said that having cancer showed him that "time is limited, so don't waste it living someone else's life. . . . have the courage to follow your heart and intuition."

These were words that Steve Jobs truly lived by. Perhaps he didn't have much time left. So once again, Steve began thinking about how to change the way people used technology.

By 2005, cell phones were everywhere. Steve had a cell phone, but he didn't like it. It didn't work well or look good. None of his friends seemed to like their cell phones, either. Steve decided to make a phone that people could fall in love with.

In 2007, at a show for new Apple products, Steve showed the audience the iPhone. The iPhone was much more than a cell phone. It was a powerful personal computer that fit in your pocket.

The iPhone made every other phone look outdated. It had a touch screen instead of buttons.

E-mail was on it; the Internet was, too. The iPhone could take photos and film action. Even though early iPhones, like early Macs, had flaws, people couldn't wait to get their hands on one.

Steve loved running Apple. But at the beginning of 2009, he started taking time off. Steve didn't admit that his cancer had returned. Even so, everyone at Apple knew that was the reason for his absence. Steve also got in touch with Walter Isaacson, a writer. Isaacson wrote biographies. Steve asked if Isaacson would write

his biography. Steve was usually very private. Yet he was offering a tell-all about his personal life. It seemed like he knew he might not live much longer. In April of that year, he had a liver transplant. Half asleep before his operation, Steve complained that the medical equipment was ugly and poorly designed!

A few months later, he returned to work. Despite his health, he had a new surprise for the public.

In 2010, Steve brought out the iPad, Apple's new tablet computer. It was smaller, thinner, and lighter than anything before it. Tablet computers had been around for twenty years. But once again, Steve made it new and different. The iPad was a portable computer with no wires. It was much larger than the iPhone so it was easy to read books on it or browse the Web or watch movies or play games. Apple sold three hundred thousand iPads in one day. In 1997, Apple had nearly gone

bankrupt. In August 2011, it became the most successful company in the world.

That same month, Steve stepped down as CEO. He was no longer well enough to continue working. He stayed at home with Laurene and their children.

Many of Steve's friends came to spend time with
him, including Bill Gates. The two men talked
about old times. Steve said he thanked Laurene
for keeping him "semi-sane." Bill said his wife,
Melinda, had done the same for him.

According to Steve's sister Mona Simpson, a
few hours before he died, Steve looked at his sister
Patti, then his children, and then Laurene.

He said: "Oh wow. Oh wow. Oh wow." Those
were the last words he spoke.

It was October 5, 2011.

All over the world, people mourned the news.
Apple stores were covered in sticky notes thanking
Steve for all he'd done. People left bitten apples

on the ground in tribute. In California, young
people placed candles in the shape of Apple's logo
on the sidewalk.

Everyone felt that Steve Jobs had changed the way they lived. He hadn't invented the computer or the mouse or the MP3 player. But he took those things and made them part of everyone's daily life. He had done exactly what he set out to do. He had achieved his dreams.

One of the first people to speak about his death was his old friend and competitor Bill Gates. He said, "For those of us lucky enough to get to work with him, it's been an insanely great honor."

TIMELINE OF
STEVE JOBS'S LIFE

1955	Steve Jobs is born on February 24
1968	Bill Hewlett of Hewlett-Packard offers Steve a summer job
1972	Steve begins attending classes at Reed College in Oregon
1974	Steve works for Atari Steve travels to India
1976	Steve Wozniak and Steve Jobs start Apple Computers
1978	His daughter Lisa is born
1981	Steve Wozniak's plane crashes
1984	The Macintosh computer is introduced to the world
1985	Steve leaves Apple
1986	Steve buys the Graphics Group, which later becomes Pixa from Lucasfilm
1991	Steve marries Laurene Powell Reed Paul Jobs is born
1993	Steve's adoptive father dies
1995	Erin Sienna Jobs is born
1997	Steve returns to Apple
1998	Eve Jobs is born
2001	Steve introduces the iPod
2003	Steve discovers he has pancreatic cancer
2007	Apple introduces the iPhone
2011	Steve Jobs dies on October 5

TIMELINE OF THE WORLD

Elvis Presley records his hit "Heartbreak Hotel" — **1956**

Sputnik I is launched into space by the Soviet Union — **1957**

President John F. Kennedy is assassinated — **1963**

Beatlemania takes over the United States — **1964**

Bob Dylan stuns the Newport Folk Festival — **1965**
by playing electric guitar

Apollo 11 lands on the moon in July — **1969**
Sesame Street premieres on TV

The first issue of the feminist magazine — **1972**
Ms. hits newsstands

President Nixon resigns over the Watergate scandal — **1974**

Microsoft is founded — **1975**

John Lennon is shot dead outside his New York City — **1980**
apartment building

MTV starts broadcasting rock music videos — **1981**

Challenger explodes seventy-three seconds after takeoff — **1986**

The Soviet Union collapses — **1991**

Dolly the sheep is the first successfully cloned mammal — **1996**

The World Trade Center and the Pentagon are attacked — **2001**
by al-Qaeda on September 11

Barack Obama becomes the first — **2009**
African American president of the United States

Navy SEALs kill Osama bin Laden in May — **2011**

BIBLIOGRAPHY

Begley, Sharon, "A Medical Gamble," *Newsweek*, November 7, 2011.

Deutschman, Alan, "Thanks for the Future," *Newsweek,* November 7, 2011.

Gladwell, Malcolm, "The Tweaker," *The New Yorker,* November 14, 2011.

Grossman, Lev, and Harry McCracken, "An American Genius," *Time Magazine*, October 17, 2011.

Isaacson, Walter, "Steve Jobs, 1955–2011," *Time Magazine*, October 17, 2011.

Isaacson, Walter. **Steve Jobs.** Simon and Schuster. New York. 2011.

Kahney, Leander, "The Best of Frenemies," *Newsweek*, November 7, 2011.

Kahney, Leander, "The Wilderness Years," *Newsweek*, November 7, 2011.

Moritz, Michael. **Return to the Little Kingdom: Steve Jobs, the Creation of Apple, and How It Changed the World.** The Overlook Press. New York. 2009.

* Sheen, Barbara. **People in the News: Steve Jobs**. Gale Cengage Learning. Farmington Hills, Michigan. 2009.

Smolowe, Jill, "Steve Jobs 1955–2011." *People Magazine*, October 24, 2011.

* Venezia, Mike. **Steve Jobs & Steve Wozniak: Geek Heroes Who Put the Personal in Computers**. Scholastic. New York. 2010.

* Books for young readers